The Book of "Ong"

An inspiring tale from failure to success

Harry Ong

AUTHOR NOTE

Every time I write, I always have one missing word in a paragraph or sentence.
My ESL teacher told me that I have a problem with languages.
I never like to study.
I'm always in the bottom of my class, I was in the bottom in during my high school years.
But now....
I am an Education and Career Consultant.
I am establishing my own institute.
And I am writing this book.

My weakness is my greatest strength.

CONTENTS

From failure to success

-- O --

Profits of this book will be donated to

BC COALITION OF PEOPLE WITH DISABILITIES

BCCPD's mission is to support people with all disabilities to live with dignity, independence and as equal and full participants in the community. BCCPD champions issues impacting the lives of people with disabilities through their direct services, community partnerships, advocacy, research and publications.

Vancouver. British Columbia. Canada

CHAPTER 1

"Work your way around"

Sometimes, people just happen to get stuck with a job that they don't like. When I was in college, I used to think that my degree would allow me to work as a hotelier. Unfortunately, life after college was not as easy as I thought it would be. Things didn't go as I expected and I had to work as a busser at a fancy fine dining restaurant just to get by. I did this for a number of years and nevergot promoted to a server. I convinced myself that my lack of English skills was the main reason why I didn't get the promotion I sought. Although I believed I had the skills to manage the restaurant, I was stuck at my entry-level position as I saw my co-workers, the majority of whom were locals, gradually move up the career ladder at my workplace. As this happened, I started to rediscover what I really wanted to do with my life. As a person who has a natural aptitude for entrepreneurship, I left the restaurant job and started my own business. After four years working on my own, my income is four times higher than that of the manager at the hotel and restaurant where I used to work.

"I always get whatever I want, because I deserve it and I fight for it"

Since I was a kid, I've always fought for something that I wanted. I'm enamored with accomplishment. People often don't get what they want because they do not struggle enough for their goal. I know my friends always say that I don't take 'no' for an answer, despite the challenges.

"Once you decide to do something, stick with it and finish it"

Often I see people decide to do something but never finish it; again it's all back to planning. The decisions we make are our goals. When I decided to open my companies in Canada, it cost a lot of money, but I developed a good plan and executed that plan. Without planning, we cannot finish the decision that we have made.

"Learning from others"

Everywhere I go I always find that there are people who are "better than me," richer than me, more experienced than me, older than me. The reason I have become who I am today, the reason I stand where I stand today, is because I have the desire to learn from every single person I meet. I always try to learn about their experiences and apply them to myself. If you always associate yourself with people who are no better than you in terms of skills, character, personality, expertise, experience, behavior and maturity, then you will never develop your true potential and your life won't be a challenge. I wouldn't be where I am today if I did not get motivation from people around me.

Be friends with all kinds of people, but learn from people who have more than you.

"Be honest and tell who you are, because people always can see"

In my experience, I have encountered many people who talk a lot about starting a venture without doing it. In the end, it's the results we can see that count.

To always act busy costs you a lot in terms of opportunity. I often forward contacts between my associates or my friends for business opportunities. But, when you are acting as if you are always busy or important, some people will not forward your contact information or offer you a job because they will be afraid that you won't able to handle the job that you have been offered. Opportunity rarely knocks twice. At the end of the day people see the results of your actions; when there aren't any results then they see you have been dishonest about your job and business and it was all just an act.

"Be nice to people because people will be nice to you"

The best example is the hospitality industry; when we are working on the floor we do not realize that our actions towards customers determine whether the customer will be nice or how big the tips will be - especially for servers; if the server has a bad attitude, the customer might complain.

I used to work in a couple of hotels, there were many unexpected situations but I always smiled and was nice to guests. They said I was the best server because no matter what, I was nice to people. Those compliments made me proud and happy that the guests are nice to me. It just will make your day.

One time I was a banquet porter for a small hotel in downtown Vancouver, and the meeting equipment was very old. Often I worked late and by myself, and while setting up for the next function, I had to move one big heavy wooden table, which I couldn't do alone. But because I was always nice to the security staff, especially when there was a party, they helped me. That's teamwork.

"Treasure your friendship because you are not alone in this world"

I often hear that you will lose many friends after you finish college and start working, but it is not true. Yes, I know finding new friends is easy in school but to find those friends who will help and listen to you sincerely is hard.

I often tell people to treasure their friendships regardless of how old they are. The old friends who know and accept your past will help you, especially in business. Often, I hear that many people got business deals easily from their good friends from high school or college.

To treasure friendships also means that we have to respect and acknowledge our dear friends who make an effort and help us with anything. Not acknowledging it means that we do not respect the sacrifices of our friends.

"A friend is someone who understands your past, believes in your future, and accepts you just the way you are."

<u>*Unknown*</u>

 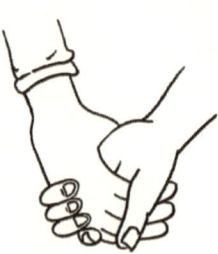

"The people that you are hanging out with are showing what your character is"

Your personality, work, and lifestyle are evident from the people you are hanging out with. My dad is a very conservative man, and our family is one of the most reputable in my city. Every since I was a kid, my dad restricted me to playing with kids only from a good family background. In fact, most of the time I went with my mom and dad to hang out with their friends. I had no choice. From those experiences, I now always choose people around me with a good family background and life direction, who are hard workers and honest – like myself. It is also a motivation to live according to the high standards of the people surrounding you. When we see a group of people or friends that always hang out with people who don't seem to have much of a future, people prone to drunkenness or theft, then the mentality of the group becomes like that. Don't associate with the wrong crowd.

One of my clients, despite his terrible past, insisted he was on the right path now. I trusted him at first but later on I realized that he was still with the same, "all-party-and-no-work-crowd," and eventually I figured out that his life is not different from theirs because he was just pretending to be better. In the end, I canceled our agreement and more importantly, even if he tried to hide it, I could still see his true character.

"Be friends with all people, but learn from people who have more than you"

I have many kinds of friends, from poor to rich, young to old, but in my life, I have always tried to mingle with people older than me, or more successful. Being around such people is a powerful motivator. Similarly, they change your perspective on goals and success and being around them will motivate you to aim higher.

"There is a time that you have to depend on people"

When I was starting my business, I always depended on people. Since then, I always promised myself to never be dependent on people, but sometimes when you do not have anything, you have to rely on others. It sucks but it is a reality that you have to deal with. Be patient and wait until you get what you want.

Sacrifice

I was looking for a job and I couldn't find one, so I offered to work for free. Yes, unpaid work, or an internship, for a couple of months. I did that solely for one reason: to learn and to improve myself. In the end, I was hired to work there full-time and this time I was being paid. And that job, I knew would lead to something big in my life.

Until I was involved in mining trading, it didn't matter what kind of position that I had as an office boy, sales, receptionist or corporate foreign affairs, director or even president. I had to use their names for networking. Sometimes working for a big or reputable company is not as grand as you might think. You have to think outside the box because the mining industry is not stable, and you have to make a backup plan. I networked with lots of financial, mining, trading companies, brokers, traders, and leaders in order to lay the groundwork for my own future company.

"A dysfunctional partner is a dysfunctional business"

Sometimes we need partners for doing business: for money, skills or connections.

Never choose partners that do not want to spend money, and with whom you have many differences in the beginning.

Don't work together if you do not like the person.

I used to have a partner in my trading company, but my partner was afraid to spend any money. Though I initially had high hopes for the partnership, I realized we were not on the same page. Then, after that, I continued on my own and eventually developed a successful career consultant business.

The next partnership was before I had my institution, I was thinking to have my former teacher whom I believed had connections in the hospitality industry. I was planning to organize a small tutorial or short training class, but apparently after one meeting, he opted to never return my calls or messages. This minor setback did not deter me from pursuing my plan; I simply changed direction and made the goal bigger: to open a college by myself.

Which one are you?

A person who likes to hang out with people on the same level as him/her.

A person who always hangs out with the people who have more experience, age, and money than him/her.

A person who likes to hang out with people who do not have money, experience.

Be the person who can hang out with all kinds of people.

CHAPTER 2

"Every single thing is vision: evaluate that vision, absorb it, adopt it as your own idea, then try to work on to it"

Once I met with a very successful person in Asia, a real visionary. He told me that all successful people are visionaries.

"The entrepreneur always searches for change, responds to it, and exploits it as an opportunity."

Peter Drucker

Stepping out from a comfortable place is the hardest part. My journey started as an education consultant, then as a busser in a restaurant. I had run my company well but in the mean time I worked there in contemplation of changing my career to restaurant manager. I worked as a busser in the Four Seasons Hotel for a couple of months and Subeez Cafe for more than one year until I finished my hospitality school. Then, I started to think that I needed to change my hospitality career. Using my education consultant connections, I expanded my business from education consultant to education and hospitality career consultant. The business went very well and in two years, the company revenue multiplied by a factor of 5, but of course along the way there were always obstacles because my clients could cut me off anytime. I couldn't just stay comfortable in case an unexpected change occurred; I had to expand it and look for better opportunities. I combined my experience in different areas into one very good business plan.

**"The biggest challenge is when you are about
to start something; the biggest success is when
you are able to survive after your start"**

When I was starting up as a school agency, it actually happened by accident. I had a person who helped me with a school contract as their agent. The duty of school agency is to promote the school overseas and you get a commission from the school because you have done the marketing for them. I was starting up with one school to reach a contract agreement and there were very few clients. From that one school I started to expand my contract work with many schools until I had many clients or future students who were looking for schools. The challenge was to adapt and learn how to deal with the schools and the students; once I did so, I started to eliminate many school contracts and keep the ones I felt most comfortable working with. It takes time to adapt and choose the best one for your company. If I didn't eliminate some of the contracts and became greedy, I might have lost lots of customers, endured major headaches and more importantly I could have lost most of my contracts.

Perfectionist

I think I can be the most annoying person, for example in restaurants. Lots of my friends criticize me because I always request a specific item for my meal. I demand perfection. I remember that one restaurant I used to like changed the whole menu. I talked with the chef and manager to explain the menu changes and the effect on taste and pairings. Apparently, they didn't listen to me and their business went bankrupt in the next 3 months. The restaurant used to be very busy and there was always a half-hour line up; that was too bad. People might be annoyed with my perfectionism but in a way it's good to be perfect; most of the successful people are perfectionists.

I am a perfectionist, especially when it comes to food because I like to eat a lot. I respect food as an art form. Taste, flavor, presentation, and cleanliness are the secret ingredients to make food not only presentable, but also outstanding and desirable. I'd like to think that all work that I do is like my food. My work and business, they are my passion and something that feeds me.

"Never listen to people who criticize your perfectionism"

"Sometimes when you innovate, you make mistakes. It is best to admit them quickly, and get on with improving your other innovations."

__Steve Jobs__

Quitter

My company is in the field of human resources and education. I have quite a number of clients. When they call wanting to quit their jobs, I always said, "Don't call me if you quit, call me if you get a better job."

I do not respect a quitter; quitters are a sad group of people. They are lazy, unwilling to venture out of their comfort zone, and run from responsibilities.

Quitting for a better opportunity, however, is a different story.

"Effort only fully releases its reward after a person refuses to quit."

Napoleon Hill

I remember the words "be careful what you wish for." When I was in high school, I wished that I could go study abroad, which I did. I thought it was beautiful to live overseas, I thought that I could be independent, far from my family and so on, but living this life was way tougher. I said to my self this is the life that I chose; I can't give up, I have to accomplish my dream. Thus, I vowed to always work harder, stronger and smarter. Effort and determination is everything.

CHAPTER 3

"Make people remember you"

A good friend of mine once told me, "Make lots of friends, make them know and remember your name."

That was a very powerful statement; we are not living in this world alone; having a network is very important to expand our names and businesses.

When people mention your name positively, that means you are trustworthy to work with. The more people talk about your success story, the more they want to come to you, but it won't happen if you never make your name memorable.

Such is the advantage of having people remember your name.

"Take a good care of your name, it is your reputation"

Our name is one of the most important parts of us, people will remember us by our name. Once you put a stain on your name, you will forever be remembered, not in the positive way, but in the negative way. Once we have a bad reputation, it hugely affects our success and business. Have your good name be remembered and known by people; it will make your work smoother.

We live in communities, which are inherently based on trust. Dishonest people tarnish their reputation forever. Who wants to do business with s cheater or thief? We want to work with good people.

I didn't really pay a lot for my school agency and career consultant marketing and advertising. I made lots of friends and earned a reputation among friends, colleagues, and their families, who spread the word, until many large schools and companies in the city hired my company as their consultant.

*"The way to gain a good reputation is to endeavor
to be what you desire to appear."*

Socrates

If I want to tell my story, then I have to write a book. If I want to have my own school program and see young students' success, then that's the time that I have to build my own school. All those achievements don't matter, good or bad can not be accomplished if I don't put 100% into it.

I have lost respect for many associates because they always insisted that they were busy, but reality said otherwise. They never endeavored to become what they desired; their "success" was all illusory, superficial, there was no substance. A mere show.

"Work hard for a better life"

Sometimes I come across people who claim that their life is hard, they can not go to school, or they can not buy this and that. I used to have little money but I never used that as a reason not to attend school. Complaining provides little of value. Hard work, dedication, and perseverance is the key to overcoming limitations. We work hard and accomplish something for a better life.

"Climb to the top"

If your life is at the very bottom, do not be afraid to scream and release all of it. Look up and try to climb again. Once you fall to the bottom of the pit, you will start to appreciate everything you once had and as you make your way back to the top, you will feel all the glory and will appreciate things more, like it's all a blessing.

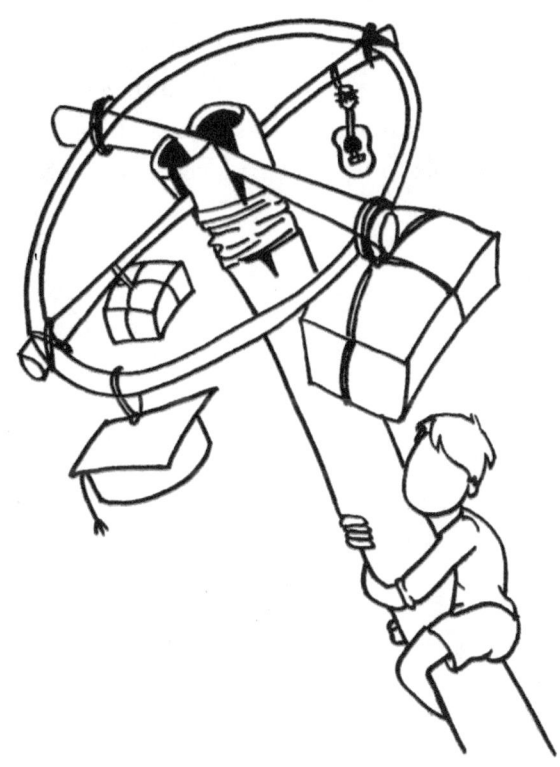

"You never know what happen next"

I have always had lots of friends and I always like to be the center of attention. Although I have finished school, I still keep in touch with my school friends. It will be an advantage to have a network of people while you are growing up, because when you are ready to enter the business world, you will definitely need a network of people; the easiest form of networking is through your friends and acquaintances. I have a professor friend in one of the universities in Indonesia. I took a long vacation in Indonesia and had too much free time. I felt like I needed to do something with my time. Right away, I got booked by 3 universities as a motivational speaker. If I didn't have those kinds of connections, I didn't think I would be able to do it. (Thank you Ms. Ayub).

CHAPTER 4

"Be a leader that listens to your employees"

Becoming a leader is easy, but becoming a good leader is not easy.

You could be a ruthless boss and your employees could be afraid of you, but there is no point in that. A good leader is a person who always listens to their employees. Good ideas may not always come from the boss; sometimes the employees or even someone with the lowest position within the company might have some ideas to better develop your company.

"A good manager is not a manager who tries to handle everything"

I used to work for a company with a manager who felt that he would handle everything best by himself, and that is not an example of a good manager.

Once you try to handle everything by yourself, you won't be able to do your own tasks 100%, because you will be concerned about other things, which are not part of your job.

A manager should be able to oversee and manage a project; it doesn't matter who will do the job or who will finish the job, but the most important thing is that the job is done correctly. The job of a manager is to oversee and supervise his/her employees, but more importantly to execute a managerial decision.

As a goalkeeper you need to be good at organizing the people in front of you and motivating them. You need to see what's going on and react to the threats. Just like a good manager in business.

Peter Shilton

"A good leader is able to see the potential of their subordinates"

Many leaders see their subordinates' potential based on whom they like or who are close to them, but that is just wrong. Good leaders always see the potential of their subordinates based on their work ethic and professionalism.

"Come 15 minute early for every meeting"

I set an alarm for myself every time I have an appointment. I always come 15 minutes early for every meeting. Your work ethic is shown through how punctual you are. If you do not have good time management, then you have to learn to manage it in order for you to be able to be a good example for others.

"Leaders are always able to make good judgments"

Many leaders lack good judgment, in my experience of observing a range of companies, from the top to the bottom. I've also witnessed much unfairness, and I've even been treated as a second-class citizen. I remember that when I worked for company that needed to sell their product and I introduced them to a potential and important client from a large company. But, in the end of the day, my manager didn't invite me to that meeting. I was a bit disappointed about it because they didn't appreciate my hard work, but after that meeting, the client, who was the VP of that company, never wanted to talk to my boss or manager, only with me. He saw that my boss did not respect me and he didn't see any point to work with the leader who can't make good judgments and be fair. That VP and I remain friends even now.

"A respected leader is a person who respects others like he wants to be respected"

Many years back when I was starting to work in the one of the best hotels in the city, I was hired as a busser. I respected the food and beverages director because the first impression when he hired me showed that he could see potential in people. I worked in that hotel for 3 months; it was very short but quitting was eye opening for me. One day, by accident, I dropped a china cup. The food and beverages director saw me and told me that if I had a brain, it wouldn't have happened. I was disappointed and lost respect for him right away, it was a very harsh comment. Then I asked myself "what am I doing here? I paid a lot for my school, I have a business running and became a busser because I was interested in the hospitality industry but I don't deserve that treatment." He didn't respect people as he should as a leader.

I moved on shortly thereafter to expand my business from education consultant to education and career consultant.

"Respect the work hours"

Good workers can be future leaders, and good workers always respect work hours. Always come early and don't cheat office hours by leaving early.

If most workers, managers and others at a workplace always try to cheat the working hours, it shows that the management system is dysfunctional.

A good company has good management, but it all starts with time conformance. Poor time conformance means the failure of the basic management system in the company.

"Practice your leadership skill while you can"

I have always been a leader; I created an association of stamp collectors of almost 100 members when I was 15. I led a school charity while I was in high school. I became a president of the student council while I was in college. These kinds of activities will always be useful; never think that it is too late start. Try to join something and take some responsibility as a leader. It's not just practice but also leadership mentality that you have to build to become a leader.

CHAPTER 5

Networking is not easy

If we want to expand our network, networking is one of the best ways to get to know people.

There are 2 kinds of networking:

Free networking is usually for the purpose of learning something or listening to a speaker. Attendees are usually entry-level management people looking for clients.

Paid networking is worth attending and spending money on. I always choose the ones related to my industry. The more expensive the networking event is, the higher the chances there will be high-ranking, high-position business people attending. The way they network is different too, but as a learner, just be confident and try to create and sell your best potential. Make them pay attention to your story and remember your name. Moreover, if they like you, they will introduce you to their successful friends or colleagues.

"How to choose your network"

Choosing the right people for networking is difficult and indeed, it takes a lot of practice. Join any associations related to your industry, mingle, sell yourself, ask the best member to go for lunch or coffee together. Sooner or later, you will learn and be able to identify who is an opportunist and who is not.

The first time I joined an association that has many CEOs of many companies, I was nervous because I didn't know what I should talk about or how to approach them. I spend lots of money on the networking and association, but maintained a goal of making five connections at each networking event. It was very hard. They are just not willing to have lunch with you unless you have something to offer. Once you have had lunch with many of them, you will learn how to choose your network and who has money and who does not.

Information

In every business opportunity, information is highly important. It makes your business easier, smother and more profitable if you know where, when, how and who to get information from.

The easiest example: I make good money in biotech and tech stock trading. Biotech and tech are not my fields, but I had good information when prices went down. I bought the stock and the value is now 40% higher. Especially if you are buying stock, information is the key to whether you will buy good stock or not.

"How much you pay, how much you get"

Networking is important. If you look for free networking, you might just get a few advantages, but most of the audience will be job seekers, brokers, insurance agents, IT services, bankers and people who are just like you. The bottom line is, you will be meeting people looking for a job or looking for clients.

If you are looking for business connections or bona fide clients, then go for networking that is expensive.

Join any non-free business association, or at least try to attend one of their events. Sometimes the events are expensive but the people who join those associations are usually important people.

I joined the Hong Kong Business Association and many other business associations in the past. I have had many advantages from the experience. I learned how to network with people, especially important people, and I had the opportunity to speak with them and improve myself. More importantly, always remember that it would make your business networking easier if you present yourself really well. You could not hope that people come to you without you having to sell yourself, but to start with, you have to know what to sell.

Publicity

Publicity for a company is key to getting know, To get publicity for your company, you must be persuasive when contacting reporters. It will be worth it. Most companies do not know how to do this and instead are just waiting be interviewed. That doesn't happen. Remember good publicity is the cheapest and best marketing.

The timing is also important. When I used to work for gold mining companies, the Premier of British Columbia went to China with business leaders to attract investors to the province. During that time, Chinese money was very hot, and lots of Chinese people came to Canada with millions and millions of dollars. I called Sing Tao, one of the largest Chinese language newspapers based in Vancouver, to write about the companies where I worked, with the purpose of introducing myself to the Chinese community, Without spending money to go to China, our company made headlines in that newspaper, read widely in Canada, Hong Kong and China. Sometimes you will save lots of marketing money with free publicity.

"Finding people who are in charge in every company that you want to be connected with is the key"

The Hong Kong Business Association, Russian Business Association, the Association for Minerals Exploration of British Columbia and Japanese Business Association: those were the associations I joined to make contacts, although my company was small. I always strove to make connections with the individuals in charge of each company I networked with, because once I needed something, I was in a position to talk directly with those people who are best equipped to help you.

I thought it would be hard to talk with the person in charge, but you just have to do your research first and then introduce yourself. Of course, your performance must impress them thoroughly. Once they are impressed with your achievements and perceive that you are an honest person and a hard worker, then it's easy to find the right contacts.

"Don't be afraid to spend your money for the right network"

For networking, I always spend lots of money for membership fees, from $70 to $600 per year and $80 to $140 per event. When I was new to business, I joined all the organizations I could. I also spent a lot on business lunches at nice restaurants to demonstrate my value and intent. If you want to spend money, then you will have a strong network and circle, which will surround you with successful people and create a good name for your enterprise but you have to spend money for it.

CHAPTER 6

"Run for inspiration"

I run sometimes for my health, but I didn't realize that while I was running, I had lots of ideas running around inside my head. They were positive ideas for sure. Sometimes running can help you to find solutions for your problems, and lift your spirits when you are down. Find good music to inspire you and find friends to support you.

I have always shared my runs with a good friend of mine.

Two of the best places for running: one is in Vancouver, British Columbia, with the mountains, weather, waterfront and things that you can not get anywhere else, and another place is Lincoln, Nebraska, USA. The place is flat and hot during summertime and there are lots of golf courses. After a run there are many swimming pools and Lincoln has many festivals. I had the best BBQ ribs at the Lincoln ribs festival. Sometime you need reward your own body. But more importantly, run for inspiration.

"There is nothing wrong with having high standards"

It is true that we have to save money, but also aim for high quality items, because when you aim for high standard items, you will have a much bigger motivation to make more money, but never buy something that you can't afford.

To be honest I do not drive in Canada. I hate driving. Up until now I have always used public transportation. But I have a friend who inspired me and he loves cars so much, especially luxury cars. He often brought me to luxury car dealerships for sightseeing, and he drove a Mercedes so he often brought me to the Mercedes car dealership. He told me he wanted me to see, dream and aim for higher standards. That way you will work harder to reach those standards of living: some people can accomplish it, some people cannot.

"Be a dreamer and fight for it"

Some people say that I am a dreamer; I am dreaming and fighting for my dream at the same time. I always get whatever I want; without dreams your life would not be worthwhile and you wouldn't have goals.

When I was a kid, I always dreamed of having my own school, my own company, writing a book, and coming to Canada. Yes, I did it all and I am doing it now. I don't care what people say, but I am proud I could pursue my dreams.

Don't be thinking of all your unrealized dreams on your deathbed; be the person who accomplishes them before, or at least fights for their dreams.

"If you listen to your fears, you will die never knowing what a great person you might have been."

Robert H. Schuller

Life is a gamble. I do not want to be a person who regrets anything before I die. I have to try everything. I have accomplished my dream.

You wouldn't able to accomplish it if you always listen to your fears, I conquer all my fears. Before I had this institution, I was also trying to get involved with the mining industry, I didn't have any background or experience, so I got involved in trading mining equipment. I went to the government small business office to find a local manufacturing company related to mining. I called the president and I told him that I want to be the distributor for the Asian market. We met and I had an exclusive agreement. Since then, my company operates as a mining equipment trading company, from there I was involved in the mining world. Besides my institution, soon the company I own will also be involved in the financial and natural resources industry.

"Earn your money with pride"

There are many ways to become rich and famous, but if you want your way up, then earn it with pride and respect. I earn my own money. I could buy anything from cheap to expensive and travel anywhere in this world because I have money and I earn it with hard work.

Some nights in the past, I simply stared at three of my friends eating dinner while I drank tea only because I did not have any money. Though those experiences were sad, they encouraged me to work harder to one day be able to buy anything.

"Try everything"

I always love doing business. I have tried everything from consulting, trading, exporting and importing - even selling food. Some of them came to be a success, and yes, some of them failed. Do not be afraid to try, because only then you will know where your passion is. If it fails, then take it as a learning experience.

I was selling diamond drills for gold mining operations, and the sales weren't that good. At first I thought it was useless, but no, those experiences landed me a job with a gold mining company in Vancouver. While working there, I learned a lot about commodity trading companies and was able to do lots of networking. I knew those experiences would lead me to something big in the future. I never think that anything I have done is a failure.

"There are no secrets to success. It is the result of preparation, hard work, and learning from failure."

Colin Powell

Success requires learning from failure. I regret none of my failed ventures since I knew each would bring new, powerful knowledge. For example, after a brief failed tenure as an employment agent who worked with an immigration consultant, I moved on quickly when I saw that wasn't working and changed directions, finding opportunities and expanding my education consultant to become a hospitality career consultant, which was very successful.

"Always Plan Two Steps Ahead"

Every plan that I make is always two steps ahead because I want to be ahead of everybody else and I want that plan to stay as my long-term investment.

"Don't be Afraid to Spend Money"

Spend money for networking, because we want to network and expand our contacts. During networking, it is important to talk with the leader of companies in your industry.

Spend money for your company. The cheaper you are cheap, the more trouble you will have in the future. Start from the beginning to have everything in order even though it will cost a lot of money.

Idea, idea, idea

An idea is just an idea if we never execute it. When I know that I have an idea, I will try to answer "how?" "How?" is our way to make that idea work.

I never think too far ahead. The first step after I find the idea. We have to try to execute it. If we never try to find the answer, or even worse, do nothing about it, it's just going to be ideas after ideas, but it's all meaningless until we put effort into it.

When we have a lot of ideas, we always forget the foundation of how to work those ideas out. One problem that will often kill an idea is money. A lot of ideas need a lot of money. Once money becomes a problem, the idea is often abandoned.

The solution for money problems is knowing the idea works. When we know that money is the limitation, the solution is to figure out how to finance that idea. If you are serious about your idea and confident about it, find the "how" answer: find the problem and try to solve it.

"There are always plans A, B, C and D"

When the Chinese government (NDRC) sent their representatives to explore companies worth investing in, there were only 10 companies allowed in to present in front of that delegation, even though about 2,600 Canadian companies, especially mining firms, expressed interest. I thought mine was too small, but nevertheless, I devised a plan. The first step was to contact the Chinese Embassy to register for a spot, then to contact the B.C. Ministry of Jobs, Tourism and Innovation. After that, I still had to find the organizer, which was Foreign Affairs and International Trade Canada, and set up a meeting with them make sure our company was on the list. Our company presented third; it was good timing because after the fifth company, usually people are too tired to listen. But it was all thanks to my all good planning and foresight.

"Do something that people never done it before"

We always want to work in the field that we want and in the best company. Every time I was looking for a job, I always did something different from other people.

I never got a call from online job postings that I applied for.

When I was buss person in the Four Seasons Hotel, I had no experience and didn't have a clue as to what a buss person was.

I got the job because I called and tried to find the head of the food and beverage division. I dropped by and requested a meeting with the Food & Beverages Director. I was lucky that the Food & Beverages director was available. He was surprised that I would ask for meeting. I could see the shock on his face.

I told him I was looking for a job and handed him my resume. It was a quick meeting but I got the job very quickly in the end.

CHAPTER 7

"The words that you say is a promise that you make"

I am always careful when I say something about work, instead of making empty promises and lavish exaggerations. People do listen; professionalism means keeping your word.

"You are your own salesmen: sell yourself and know where to sell"

The process to know where to sell yourself is hard. First you have to know about what you are doing and about yourself. Before, when I wanted to set up a meeting with a company's leader, I had to promote or market myself. One day I was eager to see one CEO from an oil and gas company. I tried to sent his company oil and gas project information for couple years, until in the end he was inviting me to his penthouse. I was amazed by the beautiful art work and especially the million-dollar Monet painting. I sat down and I told him my purpose for seeing him, and finally he told me that before I want to sell myself to him, I had to demonstrate something special in me. I was my own salesman but I didn't know where to sell because I didn't know what my product was. His word stuck inside my head until I realized that indeed I am my own salesmen, but before I sell my product I have to know about it and where to sell it.

"Nothing is easy and fast"

Every job needs a process. If you want to gain a lot, you have to go through a long process.

For example, you can make money with a shortcut, plus gain a lot from it, because a shortcut is easy. But soon without realizing it, you will always live in fear, and in the end, when the time is up or when your luck runs out, the consequences will be severe and cause you to lose more than you can ever imagine.

"One biggest mistake is always taking a shortcut"

"A rule is rule, but for every rule there is always a small hole. Find the hole without breaking the rule"

Loopholes are everywhere, a means of circumventing barriers, but how we can get to that loophole? Learning from our own observation, learning from others, or from our experience.

"Hell, there are no rules here –
we are trying to accomplish something."

<u>*Thomas A. Edison.*</u>

CHAPTER 8

"The best salesman is the one who treats their customer like a king"

I feel comfortable shopping at some shopping mall in Downtown Vancouver; despite the price they have the best customer service. Every time I come, they remember what I bought and my size and preference.

The best salesmen are people who do not care where they work; they will always provide the best customer service. If you can maintain the best customer service no matter where you work, people will always try to find you. It would be advantageous if the items are cheap and the customer service is a luxury.

"The biggest mistake of a salesman is being rude"

Never think that a customer will forget. You may think they are fine after you say sorry, but if you do not take action to apologize to your customer, they will move to another company sooner or later.

We are a professional company, and many of the leading private colleges in Vancouver use our company's services. Our company has the best customer service, we always treat our customers like kings. But we never forget to also tell the truth to our customer; we never tell lies.

Be a smart broker

The broker's life seems like a dream: party a lot, talk about millions of dollars.

There are 2 types of brokers.

A smart broker knows where to network and how to use money. They are able to spend money on joining exclusive organizations, finding the right contacts and are willing to buy lunch for any high-position person from a notable company.

A broke broker is always looking for a free party and networks among broke brokers, talking about millions of dollars which they don't have. They have a tendency to always hang out and drink with the same people from their industry. When they network with the same broke salesmen, they will spend money pretending to be rich and in the end, they just drink and talk about imaginary deals. Behind that curtain, those brokers are broke.

"Good salesmen never make stupid statements"

Once I bought shoes, and after I brought them home I realized the left shoe was wrinkled. Of course I returned it because I want something new. The salesman told me the wrinkles were fine because you will wear it anyway and it will show a wrinkle line after wearing it 10 times. I thought, "why don't I just buy second hand shoes instead?"

Customers are sensitive because they pay money for your item; never tell them what to do, always listen and find better solutions.

"A successful company has the best customer service"

I have a friend who owns a successful gold mining company, and I learned from him that he always respects their customers and investors. When your customer is happy, it doesn't matter how much money they will put into the company, because they develop a sense of trust towards your company. That's why we are always telling good stories, listening and treating the customer with respect.

"Sales are contingent upon the attitude of the salesman – not the attitude of the prospect"

W. Clement Stone

CHAPTER 9

"The best way to be successful is always be happy"

When we are happy, all the positive energy will be surrounding us, when we have that strong positive energy, people will always want to be close to us.

"The foundation of your success is being proud of what you are doing"

I am proud of my achievements, but surely at times, people denigrated them or my ventures. Nevertheless, you must ignore such criticisms and push onward.

When I tried to start my mining equipment trading company, I was proud of my efforts, and I told people that this is what I am doing. Although I had not sold very much, I still took pride in my work, which I knew would open up other avenues infield like mining or finance.

All the work that I did in the past and failed turned out to be something useful and became part of my new venture. If I never felt proud about all my work, I wouldn't be able to stand where I am now.

P.S.: I was also happy and proud that I had once worked as a busser.

The Happiest Day

The happiest day of my life is when I leave the house and I can breathe the fresh air. I feel happy that I still exist, healthy and alive. I appreciate what I have now. I can buy and eat whatever I want, and I also have my diet and exercise. Every day I keep it positive.

My point of view on life changed when I went to my friend's funeral; it was a sudden death and he had lots of complications at a young age.

I realize that we never know what could happen to us tomorrow, but we have to appreciate everything while we still can. I want to make every day a happy day.

"Happiness does not come from doing easy work but from the afterglow of satisfaction that comes after the achievement of a difficult task that demanded our best."

Theodore Isaac Rubin

"I want my name and wealth in every corner of the world - say it out loud"

Dreams and confidence go hand in hand. Many people are afraid to talk about their dreams because of fear of judgment or criticism of others. I do not care what people say - I am bolstered by my own confidence.

Always say your dreams out loud and with confidence; keeping it secret will inhibit its growth. Just be confident, work hard, and refuse to be diverted from the path to success, and eventually, you will achieve it!

"I want to put a ding in the universe"

<u>Steve Jobs.</u>

Temper and Ego

In the business world, I have to control my temper and ego. Many people just let everything go with their temper and ego, and when I meet such people, I will not have a screaming match with them, because I am not on the same level with those people. Speak your mind and let them know that they are wrong; tell them that you mean it. You will be above those people. Once you scream, you will lose self-respect.

"Never overvalue yourself"

Sometimes we think that we are better than other people; this thought will be your worst mistake. From my experience as an education and career consultant, some students who have just started their careers and do not have any experience or references, but they want to get the best job. I had a student who had just graduated and I was looking for an intern. I asked this student, but he refused. Three months later, he was still unemployed and looking for his dream job without any experience.

I myself had an internship for more than 3 months in order to get a job that I wanted, because the most important thing is to get references first; it doesn't matter in what position you have to start.

The book of "Ong"

ACKNOWLEDGMENT

I have always wanted to write a book. Without the people who have supported me, I wouldn't have been able to write this book.

I want to express my deepest appreciation and gratitude to those who have motivated me to write this book.

In the memory of Djoko Surjo, a very special person who supported me from the beginning. Mr. Surjo was the first person who believed that I could write a book and share my words with people.

To my family, who are always supportive and have always believed in me.

To the graphic designer and illustrator of this book, Hubertin Pramagita and Nathania Caroline Candra.

To people who came to my rescue during my journey: Hungga Charong, Dharmawan Sentosa and Robby Tjahyono, who know my past and present.

To Huang Lily for always giving me her wise advice.

To Luthfi Dhofier and Alexander Darryl Linardi for believing in this book and also editing and revising it.

I should extend a thank you to Jenny Wang, Meena Wong, Christian Bernard and to all those who believe in me.

ABOUT THE AUTHOR

Harry Ong is a highly sought-after international business speaker, consultant, trainer, and educator who demonstrates a deep understanding of the importance of self-leadership in business and in life.

Having created his own successful international business, Harry believes that leadership is a state of mind and helps individuals at any stage of their career to master personal leadership; that is, the ability to take charge of oneself first in any situation. Harry speaks passionately about self-actualization, the importance of outstanding leadership in the workplace, and the roles of positive communication and influence.